The ultimate business skills collection from Bloomsbury Business

The new *Business Essentials* series from Bloomsbury Business offers handy pocket guides on a wide range of business topics – from writing a CV and performing well in interviews, to making the most impactful presentations, finding the right work/life balance, brushing up your business writing skills, managing projects effectively, and becoming more assertive at work.

Available from all good retailers and bookshops, as well as from bloomsbury.com/businessessentials

Tackle Office Nightmares

How to cope with tricky situations and people

BLOOMSBURY BUSINESS

LONDON · OXFORD · NEW YORK · NEW DELHI · SYDNEY

BLOOMSBURY BUSINESS
Bloomsbury Publishing Plc
50 Bedford Square, London, WC1B 3DP, UK
29 Earlsfort Terrace, Dublin 2, Ireland

BLOOMSBURY, BLOOMSBURY BUSINESS and the Diana logo are trademarks
of Bloomsbury Publishing Plc

First published in Great Britain in 2004 by Bloomsbury Publishing Plc

This revised and updated edition published in 2023 by Bloomsbury
Publishing Plc

A catalogue record for this book is available from the British Library

Library of Congress Cataloguing-in-Publication data has been applied for

ISBN: 978-1-3994-0778-6; eBook: 978-1-3994-0777-9

2 4 6 8 10 9 7 5 3 1

Text design by seagulls.net

Typeset by Deanta Global Publishing Services, Chennai, India
Printed and bound in Great Britain by CPI Group (UK) Ltd, Croydon CR0 4YY

To find out more about our authors and books visit www.bloomsbury.com
and sign up for our newsletters

Contents

How happy are you at work?

Answer the following questions, then read the guidance points for advice on how best to deal with your situation.

How 'political' is your workplace?

a) Not very b) Fairly c) Very

How many trusted allies do you have at work?

a. I trust most people. The atmosphere is very open and relaxed.
b. I have a few very good friends at work whom I trust.
c. None. I keep my guard up at all times.

How 'cliquey' do you consider your workplace?

a) Not very b) Fairly c) Very

How comfortable are you with confronting colleagues about tricky issues?

a) Very b) Fairly c) Not at all

How high is morale in your workplace?

a) Pretty high b) Generally OK c) Low

How well do you think your managers have handled difficulties in the past?

a) Well b) OK c) Badly

How would you describe the management culture in your organization?

a. Friendly
b. Intimidating at times
c. Bullying and discriminatory

How often do you feel discriminated against, for whatever reason (gender, religion, ethnic/social/cultural background, disabilities, age, sexuality, education)?

a) Hardly ever b) Rarely c) Regularly

How often do you feel 'put upon' at work?

a) Rarely b) Sometimes c) Regularly

How do you feel about your boss?

a. I respect their management skills.
b. I feel awkward at times, but generally OK.
c. I'm not keen.

You suspect that a colleague dislikes you. How do you deal with it?

a. Speak to them to find out why.
b. Act normally and hope they get over it.
c. Try to avoid them.

How many of the following do you feel you experience regularly in the workplace: bullying, discrimination, being taken for granted, others taking credit for your work, being blamed unfairly, decisions made over your head, lack of communication?

a) 1-2 b) 3-4 c) 5-7

a = 1, b = 2 and c = 3.

Now add up your scores.

Everyone should read Chapter 1 as it offers advice on dealing with an unavoidable feature of any workplace – office politics.

12–20: While you seem to be happy at work, it is important to keep an eye out for colleagues who may be having difficulties (Chapter 7). Make sure you are aware of the legal side of discrimination (Chapter 5), and watch out for the signs of drug or alcohol misuse – you may be able to help before it is too late (Chapter 6).

21–30: You're doing well, apart from a few seemingly inescapable difficulties. You must be aware that the problems may lie with you – Chapter 8 suggests new approaches to such challenges. If you have a difficult relationship with your boss, read Chapter 2 for advice.

31–36: You seem unhappy about many aspects of your work. If you feel you are being unfairly treated, read chapters 2, 3 and 4 to determine the cause of the problem and find suggestions for how you can improve your situation. Chapter 8 suggests new ways of thinking that may help ease your discontent.

1
Handling office politics

Life would be wonderful if you could work in an office without worrying about other people and what they're up to. However, everyone has a network of relationships throughout the organization and, if you don't handle them carefully, it's possible that you could be heading for an office nightmare.

You don't have to work somewhere long to figure out whether or not is has a 'political' culture. In these organizations, *who* you know tends to matter more than *what* you know. Friendships and casual conversations take on a new significance – one wrong word to the wrong person could end up scuppering that promotion.

The context in which people have come to know each other is also important in a 'political' culture, as that can imply certain kinds of loyalty. Family, school or social networks that intrude into professional territory can embroil people in all sorts of Machiavellian manoeuvres that eventually create a politically charged workplace. If you find yourself in such a minefield, this chapter offers advice on how to pick

your way through. It also suggests ways for managers
to avoid and discourage 'politicking'.

Step one: Watch for signs of office politics

Politics plays a part in all organizations; it is an
inevitable effect of putting human beings together
in some sort of hierarchical arrangement. Indicators
of office politics are often fairly easy to pick up – just
hang around near the kettle, water cooler or canteen
in any organization.

- Listen out for clues about how the business
  works under the surface. Perhaps you might hear
  comments from people who have been passed over
  for promotion in favour of the recruiting manager's
  former golf partner.

- Watch out for those who succeed by publicly
  supporting their boss, or by ensuring that they are
  always in the right place at the right time. Such
  successes again indicate that hidden agendas may
  be at play.

TOP TIP

If you're already embroiled in a political situation,
it's important to go through the correct channels to
avoid compromising yourself further. Explain what
has happened to your supervisor or manager. If the
political situation involves your boss, you may want
to approach your human resources department, if
you have one, to ask their advice about the best
way to proceed.

Step two: Ensure your own survival

Self-preservation is always desirable, but don't use political dirty tricks to survive, whatever your level of responsibility – they will only create new nightmares. If your organization is rife with politics, you can survive by following some simple rules.

✓ Observe the organization's political style without getting involved until you're sure that you know what's going on. You may have started to notice coincidences or inconsistencies. Bide your time and watch the process so that you can begin to understand what the patterns and motivations are.

✓ Keep your own counsel during this period and work according to your own values. Don't try to change your values to match those of the organization; under pressure, your own values will reassert themselves forcefully. Remember that you can't please everyone all the time, so use your own integrity to make decisions.

✓ Build a network of trusted allies. During your observation phase you will have identified who these people could be. It's also a good idea to build a network outside the organization to create options and opportunities for yourself. This will take the focus off work for a while and gives you time to reconfirm or realign your values.

TOP TIP

Male networks have controlled the power in businesses for hundreds of years and they can be impenetrable. If you are a minority, you may find it helpful to find a mentor inside or outside the business, who will champion you and look out for information and opportunities for you. Build your relationships carefully and find ways to contribute your skills and ideas that will be valued by all your colleagues. Don't let them take advantage of your talents, though; follow up and ask for feedback. In this way, you will build the respect of your whole team and find a tenable position within it.

✓ Expose other people's politically motivated behaviour. When colleagues say one thing and do another, or seem to be sabotaging your decisions or work relationships, use your assertiveness skills to challenge their motivation: 'You seem to be unhappy with the decisions I've made; would you like to discuss them?' They will either have to deny your assertion or confront it, but at least the issue will be out in the open.

✓ Find a mentor with whom you can discuss your observations and concerns. You may gain a deeper understanding of the political processes at work and some insight into how you can manage these more effectively.

TOP TIP

If you're in a large organization but want to avoid politics in your working life, you may find that a change of environment meets your needs. This doesn't necessarily mean a move out of the organization entirely, but perhaps you could consider a move to a small-business unit or specialized department where there may be a different political culture. Smaller work units are often structurally simpler and less political than large ones.

Step three: Discourage political behaviour

In any working environment, decision-making based on politics will encourage hypocrisy, double-dealing, cliques, self-interest and deception. These must be reined in if the business is going to survive in the long term. Here are a few tips for those in managerial positions on how to create change and avoid potential political nightmares:

✓ Give promotions to the candidates who have demonstrated a relevant track record of success.

Conduct structured, formal interviews and consult with others affected by the decision. Match the successful candidate to the job description. Remember that although a good working relationship is necessary, the talents and values of the candidate don't have to match those of their new line manager exactly.

✓ Offer rewards and recognition solely for good performance, not in return for favours. All promotions or pay rises must be based on the individual's ability to reach or exceed the key performance indicators set during the performance review. Performance data should be readily available to those it concerns, with no hidden judgements or decisions.

✓ Communicate openly and transparently. Only unhealthy organizations hide information and spring unpleasant surprises on their employees. Communicate anything that affects your employees and their performance, including bad news, challenges and initiatives for change.

✓ Introduce new initiatives, projects and ideas on the basis of their value to the business, not on the basis of favouritism or possible personal benefit. Setting up a formal process for proposing new initiatives and tracing their evaluation and implementation will create confidence in an unbiased outcome.

✓ Don't be tempted to indulge in 'politicking', even when you can see an opportunity to benefit either yourself or the organization as a whole. For example, you might want to offload a member of your team in order to attract someone you feel may perform more effectively.

However, this is where the rot sets in. If you manage people on this basis, you will destroy any trust your team has in you and their performance may deteriorate.

Common mistakes

✗ You misread a situation and wade in with an accusation of politicking

At best this reveals your naivety, at worst your own politicking or neuroses. If you think a colleague is politically motivated, observe the person's behaviour until you're sure that you understand it. You may wish to share your thoughts with someone you trust or, if it serves a purpose, confront the situation. Sometimes it's preferable to leave things alone. You will be the best judge of this.

✗ You build a network purely for your own ends

Some people try to short-circuit the path to promotion by cultivating what they believe to be essential relationships. However, there is a big difference between building professional networks and using your contacts shamelessly in a headlong pursuit of your own selfish ends. Remember that if you launch yourself into an early promotion without having developed the skills to be successful, you may be setting yourself up for a very public and career-damaging failure. Build your networks prudently and use them to help develop your skills and deliver new opportunities. It may take a little longer, but it will pay off in the end.

✗ You get involved in the politics too early

When you join a new organization, try not to get embroiled in the politics at the start. Make the most of your first few weeks in your new job: your newness in the business will allow you to ask naive questions that will help you create a picture of the political environment. Keep your relationships open and friendly and build your network with a diverse range of people. Observe the patterns of relationships closely to see where the information lies and where the power sits. After a few months, you will probably have acquired a fairly accurate idea of what is going on. You can then make your own decisions about the extent to which you should get involved in organizational politics.

✗ You communicate badly

Poor communication within an organization is probably the most common cause of a destructive political culture. In the absence of sufficient information or an adequate explanation, people will fill the gaps with speculation and rumour, which circulate around the office grapevine very fast. Clear and transparent communication, leaving people in no doubt about plans or decisions, helps protect an organization from becoming a breeding ground for politics. Newsletters, bulletin boards on an intranet and company-wide meetings are all useful vehicles for disseminating information, along with more local activities such as team meetings, departmental get-togethers and personal briefings.

BUSINESS ESSENTIALS

✓ Listen out for signs of political machinations.
Informal situations can be the most fruitful for
this kind of research.

✓ Communicate openly and transparently in order
to discourage gossip and encourage trust.

✓ Don't be tempted into politicking – it's unlikely to
end well. Stay out of it and keep your integrity.

✓ Build a network of trusted allies and confidants,
both inside and outside the organization.

✓ If you must confront a political situation, go
through formal channels so that your position
isn't compromised.

✓ Try not to get involved until you fully understand
all aspects of the conflict.

2
Coping with a difficult boss

Many people have a difficult or challenging relationship with their boss. It can be tempting to lay the blame for this type of situation squarely at the boss's feet due to their unreasonable, negative, awkward or unhelpful behaviour.

Whether blaming your boss is justified or not, the good news is that, as a significant party in the relationship, there is a great deal that you can do to end the bad boss nightmare.

Step one: Consider the impact on your own health and happiness

Rather than deal with the problem directly, many people are tempted to live with the difficulties of having a troublesome boss. Instead of addressing the problem, they brush it under the carpet by looking for ways of minimizing the impact the person has on their working lives. However, employing avoidance tactics or finding ways to offset the emotional damage can be time-consuming and stressful.

Focusing on your own well-being may encourage you to tackle the issue rationally and try to reach a sensible accommodation that will prevent you from jeopardizing your health or feeling that you have to leave your job.

Step two: Understand your boss

When you come to look more closely at your relationship with your boss, the first thing to do is to realize how much of it is due to the structure of the organization – for example, your boss necessarily has to give you tasks, some of which you may not enjoy – and how much is due to truly unreasonable behaviour.

Looking at the wider issues in the organization may provide the key to the problem. 'Difficult boss syndrome' is rarely caused simply by a personality clash: more often than not, there are broader organizational factors that can go some way to explaining seemingly unreasonable behaviour.

- However uncomfortable it may feel, try putting yourself in your boss's shoes. Recognize the objectives that define their role and think through the pressures they are under.

- Make a mental list of your boss's strengths, preferred working style, idiosyncrasies, values and beliefs. Observe their behaviour and reactions, and watch where they choose to focus attention.

This will help you deepen your understanding. Very often, when we feel disliked or when we dislike someone, we avoid building this understanding and instead look for ways of avoiding the issues.

> ### TOP TIP
>
> If your boss is making work intolerable because of their moody and bad-tempered behaviour, try to work out how you could influence the situation for the better.
>
> Observe their behaviour to see if there is a pattern in it, and then try to broach this issue, letting your boss know how their mood swings affect you. Use assertive language and ask if there is anything you can do to alleviate the cause of the problem.
>
> If the behaviour persists, consult your human resources department to see if there are any formal procedures in place to deal with such a situation.

Step three: Compare the way you both perceive your role

As part of the process of understanding your boss, compare the perceptions you both have of your role and the criteria used to judge your success. You may feel that you're performing well, but if you're putting your energy into tasks that your boss does not feel are relevant, you will be seen as performing poorly.

✓ Take the initiative to explore your boss's expectations and agree on your objectives. This will clarify your role and give you a better idea of how to progress in the organization.

TOP TIP

A lack of communication often contributes to workplace misunderstandings. If you feel like you're missing out on opportunities or being denied information because you're not one of your boss's favourites, try approaching them with information about what you're doing and talk about your methods and goals.

If your boss persists in denying you the information you need, you may have grounds for a case of bullying against them.

Step four: Understand yourself

Having scrutinized your boss and developed a greater understanding of them, you should try doing the same exercise on yourself. Sometimes, a lack of self-knowledge leads to us being surprised by our reactions and the feedback we get. Ask for input from your colleagues while you're doing this.

✓ Ask your colleagues what they observe when you interact with your boss, how you come across to them, and how you could manage your communication differently. Although their perception may not represent the absolute truth about you, it nonetheless reflects the image you create in some situations.

✓ Think through some of the past encounters you've had with your boss and reflect upon them objectively, perhaps with a friend or colleague who knows you well. Maybe this situation happens over and over again, which suggests that you harbour a value or belief that is being repeatedly compromised. If you can better understand what this is, you can learn to manage these situations more effectively.

✓ Consider changing some aspects of your behaviour. This often prompts a reciprocal behavioural change in your boss. If you don't change anything about the way you interact with your boss, the relationship will remain unaltered, so this is definitely worth a try.

For example, perhaps you value attention to detail, but your boss is a big-picture person. Every time you ask for more detailed information, you will be drawing attention to one of your boss's vulnerabilities, and they are likely to become uncooperative or irritated by your request. Once you've observed your respective patterns, you can begin to work around them or accommodate them.

Step five: Remember the relationship is mutual

In order to be effective, managers need a co-operative and productive team. But in order to be part of such a team, each member needs their manager to provide the resources and support they require to do their job properly. An unsupportive boss can be just as nightmarish as a vindictive one.

When managers neglect to give their employees the information and feedback they need, employees are forced to second-guess their boss's requirements.

This inevitably leads to misunderstandings on both sides. The knock-on effects of this are an atmosphere of distrust and ill-will, and mutual recriminations – not to mention the negative impact on the organization's productivity levels.

✔ Ask for the information and resources you require, or find other ways to get these, as this will put you in control of the situation and protect you from the need to improvise.

Nightmare situations can arise when employees' needs aren't met. Some people become angry and resentful of the manager's authority; some find ways of challenging decisions in order to assert their own power; and others develop agendas of their own that are neither helpful nor productive.

One-sided relationships are a recipe for revolution! It is rare in business to find relationships where there is absolutely *no* reciprocal power. Remember that if you're no longer willing to spend time managing your difficult boss, you still have the ultimate power: you can just walk away.

TOP TIP

If your boss is making you feel miserable by constantly making negative and derisive comments about the way you do your work, you need to find a private moment when you can explain how this makes you feel and ask your boss to stop doing it. You could suggest that they give you clear guidelines and constructive feedback that will help you to meet their expectations and develop your talents. Point out that constant nagging affects the way you work and that you would be much more effective if they took a positive interest in what you do. If the negativity continues, you may decide to lodge a complaint of discrimination against your boss. If you take this route, make sure you have a record of the incidents and a note of any witnesses present. Also, seek further advice from your human resources department if your company has one.

Common mistakes

✗ You take your boss's behaviour personally

It is very tempting to take the behaviour of a difficult boss personally. However, it is very unlikely that *you* are the problem. It may be something you do, it may be the values you hold, or it may be that you remind your boss of someone they don't get on with. The only person who loses out if you take it personally is you.

✗ You don't remain detached

Many difficult relationships deteriorate to the point where they are fraught with contempt and confrontation. This is never helpful in a work setting and only makes matters uncomfortable for everyone. If you find yourself being drawn into an angry exchange, try to remain emotionally detached and listen actively to what is being said to (or shouted at) you. It may provide you with clues about why the situation has developed and allow you to get straight to the point of concern. Ask for a private review afterwards to explore the incident when feelings aren't running so high. You may find that this brings to the surface issues that are relatively easy to deal with and that will prevent further outbursts from occurring.

✗ You never confront the issue

Because facing up to difficult people is not an easy thing to do, many people avoid biting the bullet. However, this will only prolong a miserable situation. Acquiescence enables bullying to thrive and allows the aggressors to hold power. Break the cycle by taking responsibility for your share of the problem and examining what it is you're doing to provoke conflict between you and your boss. Doing nothing is not a viable option.

BUSINESS ESSENTIALS

✓ Don't neglect the problem – for the sake of your health, if nothing else.

✓ Try to see both sides of the issue.

✓ Ask for impartial help from colleagues if you feel too emotionally involved.

✓ Identify and resolve areas of ambiguity in order to reduce the possibility of misunderstandings and dissatisfaction.

✓ Don't take it personally . . .

✓ . . . but remember that you might need to change your behaviour, too.

3
Dealing with bullying or harassment

Anyone who has ever been bullied will know just how demoralizing and damaging the experience can be. When it occurs in the workplace it can be a seemingly inescapable nightmare. The effects of bullying impact a person's life outside of work and are sure to take their toll over time on the physical as well as mental well-being of the victim.

Abusive behaviours range from the extreme, such as bullying and physical abuse, to more subtle forms of harassment that are often more common but less recognized. What is tolerated in the workplace will depend very much upon the culture of the organization and the attitudes of its leaders.

Unfortunately, there are still some businesses that try to ignore harassment; but others make a point of creating a culture where intimidation of any sort is cause for reprimand or, in some cases, dismissal. It is worth reflecting on your organization's culture to see what exists, both on and under the surface. This chapter provides advice both for the victims of harassment or bullying and the colleagues and managers around them.

Step one: Understand the forms bullying can take

The recipient of bullying is often in a weaker position, physically, emotionally or hierarchically. Victims are usually unable or unwilling to stand up for themselves, due to what they feel will be the unacceptable consequences, such as an escalation of abusive behaviour or the threat of redundancy. This fear allows the behaviour to continue.

Any form of harassment can have a serious impact on the morale of staff in the business, and can affect the performance and health of individuals. Not only is it simply wrong, but it's also unlawful, and should be treated seriously.

Different forms of harassment

These include:

- all manner of physical contact from touching, pushing and shoving, to serious assault;

- prejudiced comments or jokes (e.g. racist, sexist, homophobic, ableist);

- intrusive or obsessive behaviours, such as constant pestering, baiting or monitoring a person's movements;

- tricks being played that result in risk or danger to the individual;

- group bullying, where the individual is overpowered by a number of aggressors.

Less direct harassment may include:

- the spreading of rumours, jokes or offensive personal remarks;

- written statements, letters or graffiti;

- actions that isolate the individual and prevent them from doing their work effectively;

- uncooperative behaviour or sabotage of professional objectives;

- pressure for sexual favours;

- obscene gestures and comments;

- the orchestration of situations that compromise the individual;

- manipulative 'political' behaviours, which may include bribery or blackmail.

TOP TIP

The difference between a good joke and bullying can be a subtle one that isn't always immediately noticeable. A good joke contributes to a fun atmosphere at work, and can diffuse a tense situation – but it needs to be a joke that everyone finds amusing, and isn't at someone else's expense. However, if the joke involves a person in the office being demeaned or belittled in any way, it has gone too far. Similarly, a joke that is personally critical and destructive has also crossed the line.

Step two: Determine when the line has been crossed

Often, people find it hard to know whether the line of harassment has been crossed. If they confront the perpetrators, they can be accused of 'being a poor sport' or worse. Such accusations are often used to mask what is going on, and can seriously undermine the victim's confidence.

If you are the one being bullied, the following advice will help you determine whether the harassment is trivial or serious:

✓ Seek feedback from those who may have observed any incidents. Their objectivity will help you gain perspective on the situation if you're worried that you may be over-reacting. It may be that their account gives you more ammunition to deal with the problem appropriately. Select your witness carefully though – ones you can trust to be allies throughout the ordeal, who won't 'flip' on you under pressure.

✓ If the harassment is infrequent and seems harmless, try not to take it too personally. Bullying says more about the character of the bully than it does about the person being bullied. However, if the bullying is persistent or escalates, you must confront it and report it. Even if you don't wish to face the bully head-on, there are likely to be other ways of asserting your rights.

TOP TIP

If you feel you're being bullied, but the perpetrator disguises their actions in jest, one way of dealing with this is to write down the incidents in a journal, including the context in which they took place. Ask for feedback from observers and include their comments. Over time, you will be able to see if there is a pattern to the treatment you've been receiving. Also, the record may be useful if you decide to take the matter further.

✓ Check in the employees' handbook, if you have one. There are probably procedures in place to assist you in dealing with your situation. You may be advised to report the incident(s) to your manager but, should you feel uncomfortable about this – for example, if your manager is part of the problem – you may wish to go directly to the human resources department.

✓ If you decide to lodge a formal complaint, make sure you have a record of the incidents and a note of the witnesses present.

TOP TIP

If you see a colleague being bullied and no complaint is forthcoming, you may think about intervening at an informal level. Start by asking your harassed colleague about the treatment they received. The person may indicate that they don't want to make a fuss about it and will leave it at that. Alternatively, you could speak to the bully, explaining the impact of their behaviour on the team as a whole. When doing this, use good feedback techniques. For example, begin all your statements with 'I...', and base them on events that you have personally observed.

Step three: Maintain a non-bullying atmosphere

Left unchecked, bullying can destroy the morale of valued employees and put the surrounding people into a state of fear. If you're a manager, you have a responsibility to report bullying elsewhere in the organization, even if it doesn't affect your staff. However, you don't want to create an atmosphere of persecution, either. Try to strike a balance between vigilance and freedom of choice.

✔ Bear in mind your legal obligations to your staff.

Remember that turning a blind eye to the problem may at some point make you culpable as well.

✔ Reassure staff that their complaints will be taken seriously and dealt with fairly. Most people are reluctant to report harassment because of the potential impact on their position/job. Explain what steps have to be taken, and estimate the length of time involved in the process.

✔ Give any potential complainant a few days in which to reconsider making a formal complaint. Don't exert pressure to take the issue further if the recipient decides to let the matter go – it's their choice and this should be respected.

✔ Make sure that the organization's policy manual spells out how to proceed if the person decides to pursue the charge. It will probably involve investigating the details to establish what happened, and in what context. This may involve interviews with the victim, alleged abuser and witnesses. Notes – based on facts, not hearsay and opinions – should be taken in the proper fashion and filed with the human resources department or representative.

Cases of serious assault are rare but, when they occur, the organization may not have the resources to deal with them. It may be necessary to contact a security officer or the police, and you may also need medical intervention and/or counselling for the victim, perhaps the perpetrator, and even some affected colleagues.

The incident could also involve an external third party, such as a customer. It is important to have a plan in place for such events, and then react in as calm and professional a manner as possible. The more serious the problem, the more your employees will depend on you to bring the matter to a close as quickly and judiciously as you can. Minimizing 'collateral damage' helps restore equilibrium more quickly.

TOP TIP

Once someone's confidence has been broken, they become 'easy pickings' and can inadvertently encourage bullying behaviours. If this is the case, you should still approach the victim and express your concern. If the problem persists, you would be wise to raise the issue in a staff meeting, or to report it to the person's supervisor – or to another manager of equal or greater rank.

Common mistakes

✗ You act before you know all the facts

Wading in with accusations when you think you've witnessed an episode of bullying could make matters worse: you may have misjudged the situation. Unless it's a serious incident, it's best to observe and question before intervening. In this way, all parties are given a chance to explain their behaviour and resolve the situation calmly.

✗ You mistake a genuine extrovert for a bully

Extroverts frequently speak their minds before really thinking about what they are saying – which can sound confrontational and be mistaken for harassment. By sharing your perception and inviting theirs, it's possible to clarify and dispel the situation without further entanglement.

✗ You don't consider that the bully may need help too

It is easy to assume that bullies are strong characters. Indeed, it's often to create this impression that they become bullies in the first place. In fact, most bullies are insecure and behave as they do to mask a lack of knowledge or skill. Or perhaps they are mirroring behaviour further up the organization, thinking that this may help them advance. One way of handling such a person is to offer them coaching, so that they can be helped to understand the underlying cause and succeed in changing their behaviour.

BUSINESS ESSENTIALS

✓ Be aware that there are many kinds of bullying. You may be suffering in more ways than you know or recognize.

✓ Ask others for their opinions on whether the way you've been treated constitutes bullying.

✓ If the line has been crossed, resolve to take action and assert your rights.

✓ Try to go through formal, established channels rather than confronting the issue on your own.

✓ As a manager, take responsibility for eliminating harassment in whichever department you witness it.

✓ Make it known that bullying is not to be tolerated and that complaints will be dealt with fairly.

✓ Try to have clear procedures in place to deal with every eventuality.

✓ Do not force people to complain if they would rather not.

4
Dealing with discrimination against you

Discrimination against individuals on the basis of their race, age, gender, sexuality, cultural background or physical/mental impairment is unlawful in the United Kingdom. The Equality Act was set up in 2010, replacing a number of previous anti-discrimination laws, including the Equal Pay Act 1970, the Sex Discrimination Act 1975, the Race Relations Act 1976 and the Disability Discrimination Act 1995. The Equality Act details the ways an employer can and can't treat someone.

The Equality Act lists nine 'protected characteristics' – race, age, sex, gender reassignment, sexual orientation, pregnancy and maternity, religion, marriage and civil partnership, and disability. It is unlawful in the United Kingdom for anyone to be discriminated against on the basis of any of these protected characteristics.

Everyone has an equal right to employment with fair remuneration in an environment that is free from discrimination. There are few experiences more depressing than being treated unfairly because of who you are. Fortunately, there are established ways in which you can tackle any type of discrimination and bring the nightmare to an end.

Discrimination is a huge subject, and there are many resources you can turn to if you feel that you've been discriminated against. However, the following will provide a useful starting point.

Step one: Racial discrimination

If you feel you've been discriminated against because of your ethnic background, don't wait; there are time limits for bringing a case under the Equality Act 2010.

✓ Gather as much evidence as possible and create a good record of the incident(s) along with a list of any witnesses. Racial discrimination isn't easy to prove, and the burden of proof will be on you.

✓ Seek guidance from trusted friends and professional confidants at the earliest opportunity and explore the legal assistance that you may be eligible for. In the UK, you can go to your union, to Citizens Advice, to the Equality Advisory Support Service or to the Equality and Human Rights Commission (EHRC).

Step two: Sex discrimination

The Equality Act 2010 makes it unlawful for employers to treat people less favourably in employment matters because of their sex, sexuality or marital status. This ruling also applies to transgender individuals and any person undergoing gender reassignment, at any stage of the process.

If you were dismissed for poor performance while a poorly performing colleague of the opposite gender retained their job, you may have a claim for sex discrimination. If you were selected for redundancy, you may have a claim if you can show that the selection criteria used affected one sex more than the other with no rational justification.

Step three: Equal pay

The issue of pay within the area of sex discrimination is covered specifically by the Equality Act. The Act does not cover you for being treated differently from members of the same sex, only the opposite sex.

There are two ways of looking at equal pay. Sometimes a person is paid less than a colleague of the opposite sex for doing the same job. Other times, one individual is paid less than another of the opposite sex for doing work of equivalent value.

Both these situations are discriminatory and may be unlawful. Equal pay rights apply to all genders. Equal pay legislation extends beyond just the obvious wages and salaries; it also covers bonuses, benefits, overtime, holiday pay, sick pay, performance-related pay and occupational pensions.

Examples of pay discrimination

There are several ways in which pay discrimination can take place. Here are some examples:

- A woman is appointed on a lower salary than her male counterparts.

- A woman on maternity leave is denied a bonus received by other staff.

- The jobs that women occupy are given different job titles and grades to those of male colleagues doing virtually the same work.

- Part-time staff have no entitlement to sick pay or holiday pay.

- All staff are placed on individual contracts and not allowed to discuss their pay rates.

Your rights to equal pay are set out in the Equality Act 2010. You can take your claim for equal pay to an employment tribunal at any time while you're in the job, or within six months of leaving employment.

TOP TIP

It may be that a colleague of the opposite sex to you has been receiving superior benefits, despite doing the same job and to the same standard. If you can prove that your job is comparable to a colleague's, involving the same level of skills and knowledge, then you're likely to have a case. However, you must be able to demonstrate this before you proceed to a tribunal with your claim.

Step four: Sexual harassment

The Equality Act 2010 makes it unlawful for employers to treat a woman less favourably than a man, or a man less favourably than a woman. The Act also applies to individuals undergoing gender reassignment.

You can only make a claim if the incident(s) took place at work or at a work-related function. Sexual harassment is defined as unwelcome physical, verbal or non-verbal conduct of a sexual nature. Cases are most likely to be brought as civil claims in an employment tribunal.

Examples of sexual harassment at work

These include:

- requests or demands for sexual favours by someone of any gender;

- comments about your appearance that are derisory or demeaning;

- remarks that are designed to cause offence;

- intrusive questions or speculations about your sex life;

- any action or behaviour related to gender that creates an intimidating, hostile or humiliating working environment.

Incidents involving touching or more extreme physical threats are criminal offences and should be reported to the police as well as your employer.

TOP TIP

If your boss has made even a single sexual advance on you, you may have grounds for a complaint. You don't have to experience persistent sexual harassment before you ask for help – if it's sufficiently serious, one incident can amount to sex discrimination. However, before you start a legal case, think about taking your complaint to the human resources department or to a trusted superior in the organization to see if there are any internal policies that can support or protect you and help to resolve the situation.

Step five: Disability discrimination

If you're disabled, or have had a disability, the Equality Act 2010 makes it unlawful for you to be discriminated against in the areas of:

- employment and education;

- access to goods, facilities, transport and services;

- the management, buying or renting of land or property.

The Equality Act 2010 replaces the Disability Discrimination Act 1995 and aims to end the discrimination that many disabled people face in these areas. A person is considered to have a 'disability' if '(a) they have a physical or mental impairment and (b) this impairment has a substantial and long-term adverse effect on that person's ability to carry out normal day-to-day activities'. The Act also says you must not be discriminated against because someone thinks you have a disability (discrimination by perception) or because you are connected with someone who has a disability (discrimination by association).

Disabled people have the right to 'reasonable adjustments' that make jobs and services accessible to them. Access to a workplace for disabled people is a legal requirement.

TOP TIP

Your employer shouldn't discriminate against you because you've taken a case of discrimination to a tribunal. People who helped you by providing evidence or information are also protected from such victimization. Making a complaint can be the quickest way to get the support you need. This could be raised either informally or formally.

If you can, start by raising the issue informally with your manager. Explain how your condition or impairment affects you, what you need and how they can help.

If you wish to make a formal complaint about your treatment at work, you will need to raise a grievance in writing. This should include names, dates and times, details of the complaint and evidence such as emails or witness statements.

Step six: Ageism

The Equality Act 2010 considers age to be a 'protected characteristic'. This means that employers cannot discriminate against job candidates or employees because of their age in terms of:

- recruitment and selection;
- training and development;
- promotion and succession;
- redundancy and retirement.

Step 7: Part-time workers

There is specific legislation covered by the Part-time Workers (Prevention of Less Favourable Treatment) Regulations 2000, which prevents workers from being discriminated against if they work fewer hours.

Common mistakes

✗ You're not prepared

The process of taking action is lengthy and evidence needs to be produced to back up your claim. Even when this is available, the procedures are stressful and time-consuming. It is always best to see if you can find another way around the problem. Start by broaching the subject with the perpetrator or having a discussion with the human resources department or an external source of advice.

✗ You take too long

There is now a time limit for employees to bring a claim under the Equality Act 2010 to an employment tribunal. That limit is three months from the date of the act complained of, or the date of the last in a series of discriminatory acts by an employer. The exception to this time frame is an equal pay claim, which must be lodged within six months of the end of your employment.

If you spend too long in an informal complaints resolution process with the perpetrator, you may be time-barred from raising a formal complaint. If you're not making satisfactory progress via the informal process, it may be useful to seek guidance on lodging a formal complaint to an employment tribunal. This will take some time to be heard, during which period you can continue with the informal complaint resolution process. If this is resolved satisfactorily then you can withdraw the formal complaint. If the informal process with the perpetrator or your employer is not resolved satisfactorily then you will have lodged your formal complaint within the time limit for it to be heard in due course.

✗ You're not sure of your ground

Misunderstanding a situation or someone's behaviour can lead to false claims of discrimination. It's important to be sure of your facts and do the research necessary to back them up. Although you'll have to talk to colleagues and perhaps consult with others in the organization, do this confidentially to avoid drawing attention to a situation that may not develop into a claim.

✗ You think that office parties don't count

It's a mistake to think that being 'off duty' or away from the work premises with your colleagues protects you from being accused of harassment. Under the Equality Act 2010, discrimination is outlawed in a wide variety of contexts that are related to your employment. In certain circumstances, action can be taken if it can be shown that the (social) event at which the incident occurred was linked to your employment.

BUSINESS ESSENTIALS

✓ Be aware of your rights. Check out the law by reading the relevant pages on www.legislation.gov.uk (or the equivalent for your area) or by contacting an independent body.

✓ Before you take action, consult the appropriate authorities within and outside your organization.

✓ Collect documentary evidence and witnesses to support your claims.

✓ Explore alternatives to legal action before rushing in to make a claim – but don't wait too long.

✓ Be prepared for a long process if you take your complaint to tribunal. This course of action can be stressful and time-consuming, so take this into account before you decide to act.

5
Preventing discrimination

In the United Kingdom there were more than 115,000 applications to employment tribunals in 2021, the number of cases having risen by 13.4 per cent over the past year.

Every employer should be aware that it could happen to them. For the small to medium-sized business, who may not be insured against such eventualities, litigation could jeopardize their future viability and, in some cases, result in the business closing entirely.

This chapter offers advice to managers and employers on how to avoid this nightmare by preventing discriminatory practices from entering the workplace.

Step one: Educate your employees

All employees must be aware of discriminatory issues, and if you are a manager, it's your responsibility to make sure that all relevant information is available, that best practice is encouraged and that diversity is valued. The senior managers should set the tone for this environment and their actions should exemplify the culture you want.

✓ Publish your policy on discrimination prominently in the workplace and on your company intranet, if you have one.

✓ Establish processes that will encourage the fair treatment of everyone in the organization, and review your progress regularly.

✓ Use every opportunity you can to publicize your policy, and include a clear statement of it in all company communication.

✓ Be seen to implement the policy consistently so that your employees have faith in its authority and effectiveness.

Step two: Implement the right procedures

A discrimination-free working environment should have the following policies and procedures in place:

✓ Policies and decision-making processes that are transparent so that there are no misunderstandings when decisions made *apparently* discriminate against someone on the basis of their gender, sexual preference, race, age, part-time status or physical impairment.

✓ Performance reviews that are undertaken regularly, where goals set previously are appraised objectively. An employee should always know what expectations their line manager has of them, and what level of success they have achieved in fulfilling these expectations. There should be no shocks or surprises when it comes to the performance review.

✓ Training in proper recruitment and selection techniques for those engaged in these processes as well as training in Diversity, Equity and Inclusion issues is advisable. This is particularly important for line managers – and if you state in your policy that you will train all of them in these areas then you must see it through.

Step three: Define your policy

Employers must have a clear written policy that sets out in detail what they expect of their employees in terms of their attitude and behaviour. The policy should specify:

- the organization's values in preventing discrimination;

- the rights of all employees;

- the individual and collective responsibilities of employees for preventing discrimination, bullying and harassment;

- the particular responsibilities of managers;

- the extension of the policy to relationships with customers and other groups;

- responsibilities for identifying and reporting breaches of the policy;

- what happens to those who breach policy – provide a detailed breakdown of the steps that will be taken in response to complaints.

If you're looking at discrimination management afresh it will be clear that you're not starting with a blank sheet. There will be 'traditional' systems and ways of doing things in the organization that have grown up over the years. There might also be – in larger organizations – an informal culture that regulates relationships between people. This may be deeply entrenched, and may also run counter to the evolving trends in legislation to prevent discrimination.

There have been many examples in recent years of corporate cultures that are (unwittingly) hostile to certain groups of potential employees. Organizations are increasingly being labelled as 'institutionally discriminatory'. To avoid this:

✓ Pay particular attention to understanding the full effects of the informal culture in your workplace, and to ensuring that it does not create problems. This is a difficult area: it isn't easy to change established behaviours. You can expect to come up against some resistance, which will need sensitive but firm handling.

Nor is this a problem that can simply be sorted in one go. Organization cultures and the social environment are dynamic, changing systems, where people come and go, and move across or up the organization, building relationships on their way. This means regular monitoring of behaviour will be needed.

Step 4: Define your procedures

Clear written procedures for reporting discrimination and related problems should also be in place.

These should be visibly supported and followed by managers and employee representatives.

The procedures should:

- be simple and understandable to all staff;

- be positive, focusing clearly on resolving any problem as quickly as possible;

- contain sufficient step-by-step detail and guidance to encourage trust in its use by both 'victims' and concerned others;

- be as short as reasonably possible, and contain target times for completion of each stage;

- give guidance to those implementing it so that the same scrupulously fair decisions are applied in all comparable cases;

- facilitate good record-keeping.

Step five: Know the rules

It is important to know that, as an employer, you're responsible for the actions of your employees. Keeping your employment practices within the law will protect you from expensive litigation procedures and possible payouts. Make sure you do your research – or, even better, consult a lawyer with expertise in employment law before you bring in any new policy.

Step six: Introduce new policies appropriately

Initially, you need to focus the application of your discrimination policy on a few key HR procedures. This will help integrate your new approach to discrimination with the existing corporate environment.

Here are some of the places to start:

Recruitment – recruit only on the basis of the skills and abilities needed to do the job.

Selection – select on merit by focusing on objective information about skills, abilities or potential. Seek evidence of positive attitudes to diversity in the workplace. If possible, publish your selection criteria and stay within them.

Promotion – base promotion on the ability, or demonstrated potential, to do the job, and on appropriate behaviour defined by discrimination management policy.

Training and development – encourage all employees, including part-time workers, to take advantage of relevant training opportunities, and show how the organization offers development opportunities to all.

Redundancy – base decisions on objective, communicated, job-related criteria to ensure the skills needed in the business are retained.

Retirement – ensure that retirement schemes are fairly applied for all, taking individual and business needs into account.

Step seven: Communicate

Keeping the channels of communication open between you and your employees is the single most effective way of avoiding discriminatory behaviour in the workplace. When people know what the rules are, and see that you're serious about implementing them, they will be less likely to risk contravening the employment acts.

As an ethical employer, you should let your customers know your policies on creating a non-prejudicial environment for your employees. Increasingly, stakeholders are making ethical choices about whom they will or will not do business with.

Step eight: Enjoy the benefits

Recent studies have shown that attention to discrimination can produce tangible bottom-line benefits. Consultation between managers and employees about discrimination was found to demonstrate care and respect. By encouraging discussion of these issues, and showing willingness to incorporate good suggestions, you can build considerable loyalty among your employees.

The studies reported that:

- inclusion improves financial performance;

- teamwork improved significantly;

- employees discovered ways in which they could personally contribute to alleviating discrimination.

On the other hand, organizations that paid little or no attention to discrimination were found to have:

- weaker financial performance;

- high absenteeism and employee turnover among those who felt they were victims of discrimination or harassment;

- higher error rates;

- increased accident rates, and higher claims for compensation;

- low morale and loss of reputation with customers;

- more errors in making appointments to key positions within the organization.

Common mistakes

 You don't provide clear company policies

Organizations sometimes forget to declare their attitude towards diversity, equity and inclusion until a case is brought against them. Ignorance is no protection from the law, and you must make sure that everyone is aware of your policies.

 You are complacent

The most common mistake is being complacent or unprepared – believing that 'it can't happen to us'. When it does happen, however, the damage to finances, profitability and reputation can be very severe indeed.

 You don't change company culture

Many high-profile cases have been brought against employers because they haven't embraced diversity, equity and inclusion. It's no use thinking that new entrants must conform to cultures that have existed for years. It's the responsibility of organizations to make sure that suitable practices are adopted to prevent any kind of discrimination.

✗ You think that only large organizations have to comply

Employment law doesn't take account of differences in the size of an organization, its circumstances or the market conditions. It is a common mistake for smaller businesses to ignore good employment practice with the excuse that they don't have the resources to support it. There are many online publications that make following the Codes of Practice straightforward.

BUSINESS ESSENTIALS

✓ Don't think that discrimination could never happen in your organization.

✓ Have appropriate policies and procedures in place to prevent it.

✓ Publicize your policies (internally and externally) and educate your employees. Always be clear.

✓ Enforce your policies, even in informal but work-related environments.

✓ Keep up to date with the law.

6
Managing addictive behaviour

Working with an addicted colleague can be a hugely difficult situation for everyone involved. If you're suffering from an addiction yourself, it's important to deal with the problem early on, before it becomes an issue that could cost you your job.

Some companies institute regular drug or breath tests as part of their standard conditions of employment. Given the statistics, this is understandable. Just look at the facts.

- Hangovers are estimated to cost UK business between £1.2bn and £1.4bn each year.

- Research by the Institute of Alcohol Studies suggests that as many as 89,000 people may turn up to work hungover or under the influence every day in the UK.

- The British Medical Association notes that 'four out of ten UK employers who responded to a survey identified alcohol consumption as a significant or very significant cause of employee absence and lost productivity'.

- The Chartered Institute of Personnel and Development recently noted that 'the total cost of absenteeism, lost productivity and lost output associated with illicit drug use in Scotland was estimated at £818.9 million'.

- A report by UKAT (UK Addiction Treatment) in 2018 noted that 40 per cent of industrial accidents are linked to substance abuse.

- The Health and Safety Executive estimate that the cost to industry of drug abuse is £36 billion per year in the UK.

Step one: Spot the problem

Those who have alcohol or drug problems are likely to be identified through a number of telltale indicators. Their behaviour may appear erratic or out of character, they may take extended lunch breaks, or they may suddenly disappear without giving a reason at odd times throughout the day.

Many of us are familiar with the symptoms and consequences of heavy drinking, but drug problems are generally less widely understood and are therefore harder to recognize. Many of the telltale indicators of drug abuse aren't unlike those related to excessive consumption of alcohol.

Symptoms of drug abuse

These include:

- mood swings or uncharacteristic behaviour;

- a tendency to become confused and irritable;

- the development of problematic relationships;

- a drop in work performance;

- poor time-keeping and increased absenteeism.

As a manager, if you observe these signals you may wish to arrange to meet the employee concerned for a performance review, during which you should concentrate on the behaviour you've observed and the likely reasons for these changes.

Step two: Do not dismiss the situation

✓ Never ignore a colleague's addiction or assume that there is nothing you can do. Early intervention will only be of benefit. Alcohol and drug misuse not only affect the individual concerned, but also endanger the circle of people surrounding them, and have the potential to destroy the person's career and relationships.

✓ Do not underestimate the damaging effects of drink – for the individual and for your organization. There is no question that alcohol reduces the ability to make sound judgements or decisions and increases the likelihood of mistakes through the loss of spatial awareness and control of the body. As heavy drinkers or drug users become more unreliable and their behaviour and judgement more erratic, their productivity diminishes and accidents become more likely.

> **TOP TIP**
>
> Every organization should have an alcohol policy to provide clear guidelines for dealing with alcohol and drug misuse at work. This policy will assure those with problems that they will be treated considerately and that they will be encouraged to seek help. The policy should be developed with the input of senior and middle managers and agreed by employees and their representatives.

Step three: Publish the policy

Many organizations now operate a workplace alcohol and drug policy that encourages sobriety and freedom from drugs. Prevention is always better than cure. Much can be done from an organizational perspective to raise awareness of drug and alcohol issues, so if you're a manager and you have a policy addressing these problems, make sure that everyone knows about it. Follow these steps:

- Post drug and alcohol information prominently in the office or on your intranet (if you have one) and embark on an education programme to ensure that everyone is aware of the issues.

- Outline the potential health and safety dangers to users and their colleagues. Explain that the organization sees drug and alcohol misuse in the same light as any other illness, and that it will be treated in the same way. Early identification of employees at risk should be encouraged.

✓ Publish the rules about alcohol consumption and drug use at work, and ensure that the message is clearly displayed in places where employees enter the business and where people gather together.

✓ Offer advice and assistance to those who feel they have a problem, and outline the help that is available. This could be through a combination of external and internal resources: there is a wide range of support services available, from medical assistance to various support groups and counselling services.

✓ Ensure confidentiality for anyone who seeks advice or assistance.

✓ Publish guidelines for disciplinary procedures and make clear what provision will be made for sick leave for treatment.

✓ Outline the basis on which an individual may return to the same job after receiving treatment, and what level of tolerance exists for repeated leave for treatment. Termination of employment may occur on the grounds of ill health if treatment is deemed to be unsuccessful.

✓ Make sure that a regular review of the organization's stance on drug and alcohol misuse is carried out and that the policy document is periodically updated.

Some organizations have a policy of running screening programmes prior to a final recruitment decision; others periodically repeat these during employment. These checks are especially important if the company's products, services or methods are highly confidential, characterized by complex processes, or performed in an environment where physical safety can be an issue. However, be aware that employees must consent to screening. See www.hse.gov.uk for more information on how to carry out screening effectively and legally.

TOP TIP

Health and safety legislation demands that employers provide and maintain a safe working environment. If incidents occur as a result of alcohol or drug abuse, both employer and employee could be liable under drug and alcohol legislation. Employment law requires employers to treat dependency as a form of sickness. This definition enables the employee to seek treatment to overcome the problem.

Step four: Act sensitively

The people who suffer most – and who notice the problem first – are always those closest to the misuser. It is therefore likely that, if you encounter this problem, the individual concerned will be a friend or close colleague. You might prefer to talk to them on a personal level before addressing matters in a professional context. If you decide to broach the subject, do so with extreme tact. The individual is likely to react defensively to your concern, and you must not become too embroiled yourself.

 If you witness a friend or colleague drinking excessively or under the influence of drugs, intervene. This may be a simple action such as calling a taxi to take the person home. Although this may feel intrusive, at least it won't result in any physical damage being done.

✓ Try talking to your friend when they have returned to full control to find out if they are aware that they may have a problem and ask them if you can help.

✓ Offer support, but avoid the role of counsellor. Helping someone manage an addiction requires professional expertise. The journey to recovery is often rocky and prolonged, and by taking on too much responsibility you could jeopardize a good friendship.

✓ Talk to your colleague's manager or to the human resources department. Don't think of it as being sneaky or telling tales but as a sign of concern for their welfare.

TOP TIP

If you suspect a team member's work is suffering because of problems with alcohol, arrange a meeting with them to share your concerns. Do not mention your suspicions at this stage; rather give the person an opportunity to allay your fears without becoming defensive. You could explore possible work-related causes to see if you can elicit an explanation that puts your mind at rest. Failing this, you may want to discuss the organization's alcohol policy and offer further assistance.

Common mistakes

✗ You leave it too long before taking action

Tackling substance misuse is difficult, but avoiding the problem only makes the situation worse for the individual and their colleagues, so it's important not to let things drift on. Besides, inaction sends a powerful message to others, who may overindulge because they believe that the organization doesn't take substance misuse seriously. If you're a manager dealing with an individual, ask for an interim performance review meeting and explore the reasons behind the behaviours you've observed. Once these are out in the open, the next logical step is to provide the right kind of help.

✗ You don't call in professional help

Being a supportive friend to drug or alcohol misusers may not serve them well in the long run and is no substitute for professional help. Dealing with addiction is a complicated business and should be facilitated by a trained counsellor. There may be someone in the human resources department (if you have one), who has experience of this form of counselling, but there are also many high-quality external resources that can assist.

✗ You fail to provide a clear policy

Organizations often don't consider drawing up an alcohol or drug policy until they actually have to deal with someone for whom drugs or alcohol have become a problem. As these forms of addiction are increasingly commonplace, it's a good idea to ensure everything is in place to deal with the problem, should it arise. The ground can be prepared through the dissemination of information about alcohol and drug abuse. This also signals the organization's intention to treat the matter of drug and alcohol abuse seriously – and may prevent some cases from developing in the first place.

BUSINESS ESSENTIALS

✓ Have a widely published policy on substance misuse *before* problems arise.

✓ Be aware of the symptoms of drug or alcohol misuse and the difference between them.

✓ Don't accuse a colleague of addictive behaviour without investigating other possibilities first – there may be a more innocent explanation.

✓ Remember that addiction is an illness and should be treated as such.

✓ Never ignore addictive behaviour. The longer it goes on, the more of a nightmare it becomes for everyone concerned.

✓ Bring in professional help at the earliest opportunity – don't try to counsel the individual without proper training.

7
Managing poor performance

Given the cost of recruitment, it's always worth trying to help an individual to develop from poor to acceptable performance. Effective management of results – particularly from poor performers – is crucial. However, it can feel awkward or embarrassing to discuss a team member's weaknesses, so such issues can sometimes go unchecked until they affect the rest of the business. This chapter will help you to end poor performance nightmares before they begin.

Reasons for poor performance

Poor performance can result from many causes, including the following:

- inability to manage perception or pressure;

- failure to prioritize;

- lack of skill, knowledge or motivation;

- conflict of personalities or styles;

- over-promotion (often termed 'the Peter Principle'), where the person is actually out of their depth;

- lack of resources, support or co-operation from others in the organization;

- change in systems or processes.

Step one: Use performance management systems

Frequently, by the time the poor performance has been identified, the damage has already been done. Prevention is better than cure, so establishing performance management systems – structured methods of identifying and improving poor performance – is ideal. These require that each individual has clear objectives, understands how these affect others, is aware of what is needed to deliver the objectives, and is confident that they have the necessary skills and experience.

✓ Put these systems in place *before* problems ever arise. It will save considerable management time and worry.

TOP TIP

Managing poor performance can be highly time-consuming, particularly when you want to be spending time supporting stronger performers. The first step is to make sure that you understand why a group is consistently failing to meet its targets.

Then you need to set clear and attainable goals and monitor their progress at regular intervals in a consistent manner. Finally, make sure that you're prepared to manage the consequences if they continue to underperform.

Step two: Define poor performance

Poor performance is defined by a range of factors. It's important that a manager can decipher which are conduct issues and which are capability/competence issues, as each will likely require a different course of action.

Conduct

- Lateness, absenteeism;
- Attitude;
- Bad language;
- Discrimination;
- Negligence or abuse of company property;
- Abusive behaviour to colleagues, managers or customers.

Capability/competence

- Failure to carry out tasks reasonably;
- Failure to perform duties to an adequate standard;
- Failure to provide high standards of customer care;
- Unsatisfactory references;

- Infringement of regulations;

- Failure to observe company policies and procedures.

Step three: Follow disciplinary procedure

Your organization must act with consistency and fairness and, where possible, be able to show that it has provided guidelines and coaching to achieve the desired actions and behaviour from its staff.

If a performance problem fails to be resolved, you may need to follow a disciplinary procedure. Here are a few useful guidelines.

- Carry out a full investigation and ensure that all evidence is well documented.

- Hold a formal hearing. Make sure the employee is given written notice of it. The employee is entitled to representation.

- Review all evidence. Formally outline the disciplinary action to be taken.

- Consider separating out conduct and capability issues, as many organizations do when undertaking disciplinary action. In the case of capability, the employee is given two chances to improve. However, if the problem is one of conduct, the process is less lenient. It is important to build in time to improve as part of the disciplinary process.

In any situation, prevention is the preferred option. However, where this isn't possible the manager needs to:

- be fair and unbiased at all times;

- behave consistently;

- pay personal attention to the matter;
- understand whether it's a conduct or capability/ competence issue;
- work within the guidelines and procedures if it reaches the stage of disciplinary action;
- recognize the importance of training and guidance.

Step four: Take preventative measures

An important part of building a team is ensuring that everyone is in a role that matches their skills and capabilities, and that each team member knows what they are trying to achieve. This should minimize the problem of poor performance.

- ✓ Communicate clearly. Leaders need to make explicit the goals of the business; managers need to break these down so that individuals understand how their targets relate to the overall business, and therefore how important their contribution is.

- ✓ Don't over-promote people. Just because someone does a great job at one level does not necessarily mean that they can tackle the next level.

- ✓ Ensure that managers are spending time with individuals to identify areas of risk before they affect performance.

- ✓ Don't overestimate goals and objectives. Optimistic management can be detrimental.

- ✓ Be aware of the culture of the business and ensure that goals are set appropriately.

TOP TIP

Restructuring can adversely affect individual performance. People often take time to adjust to new situations, and some cope with change better than others. If someone you manage is struggling with the switch, talk to them and explore exactly what differences the change has made to their working life.

This kind of problem often emerges when communication is poor, which can make it difficult for someone to prioritize or understand what needs to be done – as well as making them feel they have no support. You may need to help build the necessary new relationships, provide more support and be clear about their priorities.

Step five: Monitor your own performance

It's all very well dealing with other people's failings – but what about your own? Sometimes, you may need to admit that you're not doing as well as you could be. An honest examination of your performance might well reveal areas for improvement.

- Establish your limits. Where you feel that you don't have the skills, experience or knowledge to achieve the objectives set for you, ask for help before it becomes a performance management issue.

- Try to understand why you haven't met the objectives. What support would help you improve your performance? If the goals aren't clear, ask for them to be redefined so that you can work towards them and manage the expectations of others.

✓ Consider your attitude. How do others react to your behaviour? Remember that what works in one culture doesn't always move easily to others. *How* you say something is as important as *what* you say. Try to identify friction points before they become serious performance issues.

✓ Monitor your level of motivation. We can often outgrow roles, or find we need different challenges to feel rewarded. Work with your boss or senior colleagues to understand why you feel unmotivated. What type of recognition or appreciation would help? Explore whether the pressures in the role have changed, or whether you have different life goals. Sometimes when our circumstances change, the expectation we have of ourselves also changes. Remember that it's more cost-effective for organizations to re-motivate and align an existing employee than to recruit, train and develop a new one, so your managers will want to keep you.

Common mistakes

✗ **You over-react and ignore external factors**

When you deal with poor performance, remain unbiased, fair and consistent. Always explore why it has occurred and what could have contributed to it. Is it part of a pattern, or is it a one-off situation that is likely to be easily resolved? Over-reacting to situations isn't good for the employee, for you or for the organization.

You set the bar too high and objectives aren't explicit

It's important, when setting goals, to make sure that they are clearly defined and achievable. Remember that different people have different capabilities. Check that your expectations fit with the culture of the business (some businesses have cultures where expectations are set higher than reality – so failing to meet explicit goals is forgiven).

Set clear, short process milestones, so that you can quickly recognize where performance may slip. Most important of all, communicate regularly. Performance targets discussed at the beginning of the year and then measured at the end may not be appropriate for everyone.

You do not address poor performance early enough

Performance needs to be measurable. The easier it is to measure, the easier it is to manage. Checks need to be made at regular intervals to understand how close an individual is to achieving, or not achieving, targets. Schedule regular reviews and encourage employees to monitor their own performance. Ask them to rate their progress and suggest ways in which they could improve. Managers often set objectives and leave people to it – but if the goals aren't met, it can be critical for the business. Good performance management ensures that possible failure is identified early on and the risk is managed appropriately and effectively.

✗ You expect instant results from a series of coaching sessions

If someone is performing poorly, it's not usually appropriate simply to prescribe coaching and hope for the best. Coaching isn't a magic wand for turning poor performers into good performers – it's better used as a proactive tool to develop a potentially good performer. Confirm first that the individual has the capability to fulfil their role, then identify what needs to be done to help them succeed. Coaching in this context is then positive and motivational. Often, it's a good idea to give employees in new roles increasingly demanding performance measures until they have settled in. Always make sure you build in a fair amount of time for the employee to make the necessary improvements.

✗ You confuse personality clashes with poor performance

Personality clashes are difficult to deal with and, if coupled with poor performance, can become highly charged. Where issues may be personality-driven, bring in an impartial third party to 'referee'. Separate out the issues and look at different ways of dealing with them. Resolving one may well have knock-on effects on the others. In some cases, poor performance may be a perceived rather than a real problem. This can happen when there is a difference in understanding between a manager and their subordinate: they may, for example, each go about tasks very differently, but no less effectively.

BUSINESS ESSENTIALS

- Measure performance at all times – and make sure every team member knows what constitutes good and bad performance.

- Set clear and achievable targets.

- Offer feedback and ask for progress reports at regular intervals.

- Be unbiased.

- Ensure that the correct procedures are in place to deal with poor performers of all types.

- Match people to their roles. Don't expect coaching to magically turn an unsuitable person into a top performer.

- Make sure you're not a poor performer yourself.

8
Thinking around problems

New ways of thinking can help you solve problems before they become nightmares. It is known that exercising the brain in a variety of ways allows us to expand into unused capacities.

Our thinking styles develop over the years and become habitual – particularly those we form as we pass through the education system, which tend to focus on the skills of analysis. So when people make statements like 'I'm not creative' or 'I'm not really a thinker', all this means is that they haven't been introduced to, or adopted, different ways of using their minds.

A situation only seems nightmarish when you can't see a way round it. A more open-minded approach could give you a simple solution.

Can one process solve every problem?

In most situations, it's a good idea to allow people to understand problems and then solve them in their own way. However, using tried-and-tested techniques of problem solving – ones that are plainly mapped out and used uniformly – allows others to understand the problem and the areas

---

being explored. The process ensures that everyone involved has the opportunity to actively participate in solving the problem at any stage.

While problems *are* always different, there are some common approaches and processes for solving them. Problems can be diagnosed and the various elements identified, whether you're talking about problems in the post-room, a manufacturing roadblock or an IT systems failure.

The key is to think *before* you act. The best way to turn a minor problem into a major nightmare is to implement a solution without first thinking through the implications.

Step one: Identify the problem

Understanding a problem requires an ability to see it in its entirety – in breadth, depth and context. Here are a number of ways to evaluate the scope of a problem:

Recognition – can you see or feel the problem? Is it isolated, or part of a bigger problem?

Symptoms – how is it showing itself?

Causes – why has it happened?

Effects – what else is being affected by it?

The task then is to break the main problem down into smaller problems, in order to determine whether you're the right person or team to handle it. If not, you need to transfer the problem-solving process to those better equipped to deal with it. If the answer is yes, ask additional questions, including: Do you have the right resources? What are some of the obstacles? What is the anticipated benefit? Once you get answers, move on to the next step.

Step two: Gather data

There are two important questions here: what do you need to know, and how are you going to get it? Most information can be accessed, but there are often time and resource issues involved in this process. Data collection involves investigating the symptoms, the underlying causes and/or the overall effects of the problem. Each may have different implications with regard to how the problem is viewed. Data-gathering techniques include:

- workflow analysis;
- surveys and questionnaires;
- flow charts;
- group and/or one-to-one interviews.

Step three: Think systematically

With the mass of information available these days, the following techniques can be useful to determine what is important and how best to make sense of it.

SWOT analysis

This is used to identify strengths and weaknesses and to examine the existing opportunities and threats. Answering questions in each of the four areas enables you to think systematically about a problem and potential solutions.

Say, for example, your main headache at work was about the launching of a new product in a tricky market. The SWOT analysis could work as follows:

Strengths: What are the advantages of your new product to the public? What are the features that distinguish it from rival products?

Weaknesses: Where are the areas of vulnerability in the product? Is the price a barrier? What could be improved? Would different product features make it better? What are the known vulnerabilities in the market? Is the product launch time-sensitive?

Opportunities: Where are the opportunities in terms of technology, markets, policy and social trends? Have you got a new commercial idea or have you found a new way of doing things? Can you capitalize on what rivals did wrong?

Threats: What barriers do you face? Is your target market right? Are you facing a change in regulations? Should you wait until it's official? Is the competition stealing a march on you? Are there threats to your financial situation? Should you try to raise money now or wait for a better time?

Decision trees

Decision trees allow decisions to be made in situations where there is a great deal of information to sift through. They create a framework in which you can examine alternative solutions and their impact.

✓ Start your decision tree on one side of a piece of paper, with a symbol representing the decision to be made.

Different lines representing various solutions open out like a fan from this nexus. Additional decisions or uncertainties that need to be resolved are indicated on these lines and, in turn, form the new decision point, from which yet more options fan out.

Critical path analysis

This is another way of approaching complex projects. It allows you to determine when certain activities should be completed, so that a project may finish on time and on budget. The essential concept behind it is that some activities are dependent on others being completed first (sequential), and others may be completed more or less at any time (parallel). The ordering of these activities creates the critical path through the project.

Mind maps

Developed by Tony Buzan, these are graphic tools used to represent whatever is on your mind. They help you get everything down on paper, with no initial emphasis on ordering or prioritizing. They could be a useful first step in seeing how the land lies and identifying throughways.

✓ Start with a circle on a large sheet of paper. Inside the circle put the word or picture that best represents the idea you wish to explore. Then place other words – perhaps in smaller circles – around the hub. Let your mind wander, and bring in a galaxy of associated words and images. Finally, connect the circles with lines, accenting similar themes with colours or symbols. Once everything is down, you can study how the various 'satellites' relate to the hub, and how you want to apply the content to your personal goals.

Step four: Think creatively

Techniques that extend our thinking into the more creative realms include the following.

Brainstorming

This is a well-known technique for generating options, where every idea submitted is treated positively. This 'anything goes' approach often stimulates the presentation of viable ideas that wouldn't otherwise have been thought of. It is only in the final stages, when all ideas have been collected, that the honing and prioritizing process begins.

TOP TIP

In meetings where brainstorming isn't part of the agenda, there often isn't time to indulge someone's creative effort. However, people who come up with off-the-wall suggestions may get frustrated if you have to rein them in. Explain what kind of thinking you're looking for in that particular setting, and offer them another context in which they can freewheel helpfully. Many companies have research and development departments that encourage off-the-wall thinking.

Questioning

Ask why a problem is occurring, and then ask again
– four more times. This allows you to drill down and
get to the heart of the matter. Alternatively, ask the
six universal questions to explore the full extent of a
problem: What? Where? When? How? Why? Who?

Six thinking hats

This is a powerful technique developed by lateral
thinking pioneer, Edward de Bono. Allocate each
individual a series of imaginary hats, which represent
different outlooks, according to colour. This forces
people to move into different modes of thinking. White
hats focus on the data, look for gaps, extrapolate
from history and examine future trends. Red hats use
intuition and emotion to look at problems. Black hats
look at the negative and find reasons why something
may not work. If an idea can get through this process,
it's more likely to succeed. Yellow hats think positively.
This hat helps you to see the benefits of a decision.
Green hats develop creative, freewheeling solutions.
There is no room for criticism in this mode; it's strictly
positive. Blue hats orchestrate the meeting – you're in
control in this hat. Feel free to propose a new hat to
keep ideas flowing.

Step five: Weigh up potential solutions

Taking time to identify the most appropriate solution
from your range of options is very important.
Suggestions need to be winnowed down to a shortlist,
containing only the most realistic possibilities. To do
this, set some hard measures.

✓ Try to determine the costs and benefits of the suggested solutions. If, for example, you feel that outside investment is needed to solve a particular problem, work out the payback period. You can then assess whether your senior management team will accept it.

✓ Analyze each potential solution in turn. Force field analysis is useful for this. By looking at the forces that will support or challenge a decision (such as finances or market conditions), you can strengthen the pros and diminish the cons. Draw three columns, and place the situation or issue in the middle. The pros push on one side, and the cons push on the other. Allocate scores to each force to convey its potency. This allows you to measure the overall advantages and disadvantages of any given action.

The chosen solution needs to meet some key criteria.

Do you have the necessary people, money and time to achieve it? Will you get a sufficient return on investment? Is the solution acceptable to others involved in the situation? Draw up:

- a rationale of why you've reached your particular conclusion;

- a set of criteria to judge the solution's success;

- a plan of action and contingencies;

- a schedule for implementation;

- a team to carry out, be responsible for and approve the solution.

Step six: Put the chosen solution into action

Implementation means having action plans with relevant deadlines and contingencies built in. Any implementation needs constant review, and the implementation team needs to make sure they have the support of relevant management.

Keep asking:

- are deadlines being met?

- are team members happy, and is communication strong within and from the team?

- has the team been recognized for their achievements?

- are the improvements measurable?

- is the situation reviewed regularly?

Step seven: Measure success

All experience can be valuable in terms of adding in-house knowledge and expertise. So, ask yourself two important questions:

How well did it work?

What did we learn from the process?

- Think of creating a case study that can be shared with others – either at a conference or directly.

- Canvass people's opinions regarding the effectiveness of the process and its outcome. Ask for improvements that could be incorporated into a second phase.

Don't be scared of involving your clients in any evaluation; this can convey a positive message if handled properly, and builds trust in your ability to troubleshoot problems and implement solutions.

Common mistakes

 You tackle too large a problem

Don't take on problems that lie beyond the control and scope of the team. People often tackle problems that are too general – focus on what is specific and achievable.

 You assume everyone thinks like you do

To be productive in groups, you need a diverse range of ways of contributing. Look around you at work; you'll probably recognize different thinking styles and recall how those have led to better clarity in decisions and outcomes. Get representatives from different parts of the business to give a different angle on the problem.

You are critical of others' creativity

Under pressure, it's easy to think: 'The last thing I need is flaky ideas when I've got a deadline!' But when you're not stressed, you've probably seen the immense value that creativity can bring. Try not to stifle creative thought; rather, guide and control it openly and positively.

 You get too used to a lack of structure

Entrepreneurial businesses are often formed as a result of an extraordinarily creative mind.

However, focused thinking and systems thinking will be necessary for good decision-making and management. For a business to grow, the creative thinkers will have to accommodate the practical, analytical thinkers.

✗ You get carried away by the process

Often, when running workshops, the process becomes more important than the ideas and intellectual discussion. Don't try to use too many techniques. Getting the balance right between understanding the problem and finding imaginative solutions requires strong facilitation.

BUSINESS ESSENTIALS

✓ Remember that a 'nightmare' is just a problem you haven't found a solution for yet.

✓ Thinking styles develop over the years and become habitual, so use your untapped mind potential by thinking in different ways.

✓ Analyze the situation and determine what is important by looking at strengths and weaknesses and examining existing opportunities and threats.

✓ Explore alternative solutions by using graphic representations, like decision trees and mind maps, that let you explore your ideas more fully.

✓ Extend your thinking into the more creative realms by brainstorming and fostering different perspectives and points of attack. Question why a problem is occurring and ask more questions to get to the heart of the matter.

✓ In a group situation, let each member take on a different outlook to force new modes of thinking: emotional, positive, negative, creative and factual.

✓ Assess the impact of the solution and identify areas for improvement in your future problem-solving processes.

Where to find more help

Office Politics: How to Thrive in a World of Lying, Backstabbing and Dirty Tricks

Oliver James

London: Ebury, 2014

288pp

ISBN: 9780091923969

A fascinating deep-dive into the modern office, examining how promotion and politics work and highlighting how to survive instead of suffer.

HBR Guide to Office Politics

Karen Dillon

Brighton, Mass.: Harvard Business Review Press, 2014

208pp

ISBN: 978-1625275325

Don't let office politics distract you from your career. Learn how to navigate the nightmares with calm and integrity. A clear-sighted guide from the respected Harvard Business Review.

Your Rights at Work: A Complete Guide to Employee Rights and Employer Responsibilities

Trades Unions Congress

London: Kogan Page, 2021 (6th edition)

208pp

ISBN: 978-1398603905

Where better to go for information about employee rights than the organization that works to protect them? A respected and detailed guide that will help employees, employers and human resources departments.

Bullying at Work: How to Confront and Overcome It

Andrea Adams

London: Virago, 1992

256pp

ISBN: 185381542X

Based on more than three years' research by the author into this theme, this book investigates the psychological make-up of the workplace bully. Aimed at both people who have been bullied and companies who may have to face up to the problem within their workforce, this book offers practical advice on how to overcome this growing problem.

Managing Your Boss in a Week

Sandi Mann

London: John Murray Press, 2016

128pp

ISBN: 978-1473607873

Divided into seven chapters (one for each day of the week), this book sets out to help you develop a partnership with your boss, so that poor communication and resulting antagonism can be improved. It offers advice on how to understand your boss, how to improve your relationship, and how you can impress them.

UK government legislation

www.legislation.gov.uk

Equality and Human Rights Commission

www.equalityhumanrights.com/en

Health and Safety Executive

www.hse.gov.uk

Diversity

https://www.mckinsey.com/featured-insights/diversity
-and-inclusion/diversity-wins-how-inclusion-matters

https://www.bbva.com/en/why-diversity-and-inclusion
-are-good-for-the-bottom-line/

Alcohol and drugs at work

https://www.hse.gov.uk/alcoholdrugs/screening
-testing-drugs-alcohol.htm

https://www.ias.org.uk/news/hangovers-cost-the-uk
-up-to-1-4bn-a-year/

https://www.bma.org.uk/media/1067/bma_alcohol-and
-drugs-in-the-workplace-_oct_2019.pdf

Index